OUR GREAT STATES

WHAT'S GREAT ABOUT
WASHINGTON?

✳ Mary Meinking

LERNER PUBLICATIONS ✳ MINNEAPOLIS

CONTENTS

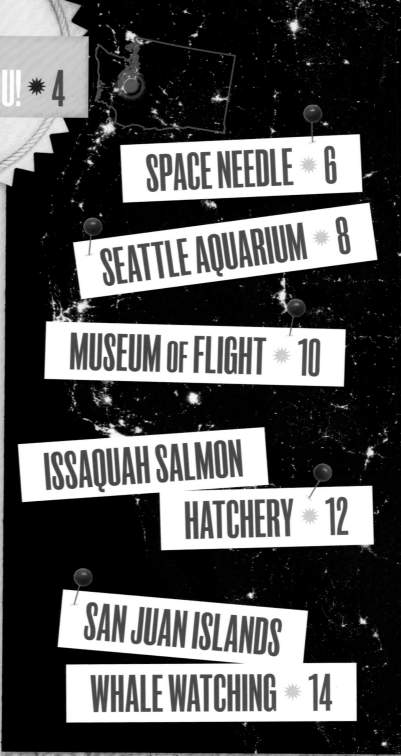

WASHINGTON WELCOMES YOU! ✳ 4

Content Consultant: Brian Casserly, Professor of History, Bellevue College

Lerner Publications Company
A division of Lerner Publishing Group, Inc.
241 First Avenue North
Minneapolis, MN 55401 USA

For reading levels and more information, look up this title at www.lernerbooks.com.

Main body text set in ITC Franklin Gothic Std Book Condensed 12/15.
Typeface provided by Adobe Systems.

Library of Congress Cataloging-in-Publication Data

Meinking, Mary.
    What's great about Washington? / by Mary Meinking.
        pages   cm. – (Our great states)
    Includes index.
    ISBN 978-1-4677-3865-1 (lib. bdg. : alk. paper)
    ISBN 978-1-4677-6267-0 (eBook)
    1. Washington (State)—Juvenile literature. I. Title.
F891.3.M47 2015
979.7–dc23   2014018043

Manufactured in the United States of America
1 – PC – 12/31/14

WASHINGTON Welcomes You!

Welcome to Washington, the Evergreen State! Washington was named after the United States' first president, George Washington. It is the only state named after a president. Washington's nickname comes from its many evergreen forests. But that's not all Washington is known for. The state is home to steaming volcanoes and rocky shores. Venture into soggy rain forests or parched deserts. See Seattle's famous Space Needle. Catch a glimpse of orca whales on a whale-watching tour. Read on to learn about ten things that make Washington great!

CANADA

ROCKY MOUNTAINS

Strait of Juan de Fuca

Puget Sound

Miles
0   20   40   60
0   40   80
Kilometers

Port Angeles

OLYMPIC MOUNTAINS

Everett

Seattle

Bellevue

Renton

Kent

Olympia

Tacoma

Columbia River

N

COLUMBIA PLATEAU

Spokane River

Spokane Valley

Spokane

IDAHO

Mount Rainier
(14,410 feet/
4,392 m)

CASCADE RANGE

Yakima

Snake River

PACIFIC OCEAN

Columbia River

Vancouver

OREGON

Walla Walla

BLUE MOUNTAINS

Explore Washington's
waters and all the places in
between. Just turn the page
to find out all about the
EVERGREEN STATE. >

SPACE NEEDLE

Catch a great glimpse of Puget Sound from atop the Space Needle.

> Seattle is Washington's largest city. Here, the famous Space Needle stands tall above the other buildings. The Space Needle building looks like a flying saucer atop a tower. It was built for the 1962 World's Fair. The building helped show off US technology to the world. A glass elevator shoots you up 520 feet (159 meters) to the observation deck. From there, you can enjoy the 360-degree view. Peer through the telescopes to see mountains in the distance. Or check out the ant-sized people and cars below.

If you're hungry, stop on the level below the observation deck. Here, the SkyCity restaurant slowly rotates. It makes a complete circle every forty-seven minutes. Try the Lunar Orbiter ice cream sundae. A cool cloud of dry ice rises from this frosty treat! Once you're back on solid ground, hop aboard another World's Fair attraction. The Seattle Center Monorail looks like a glass bubble train. The 1-mile (1.6-kilometer) trip to downtown Seattle takes just two minutes.

The Seattle Center Monorail glides above the streets at 45 miles (72 km) per hour.

SEATTLE AQUARIUM

> Have you ever wanted to go under the sea? If so, the Seattle Aquarium is the place for you! Come face-to-face with sea creatures. You can view them in the 400,000-gallon (1.5 million-liter) Underwater Dome. You'll feel as if you're inside a fishbowl! Watch sharks and schools of fish swim around you. Be sure to check out the giant Window on Washington Waters tank. It's filled with more than eight hundred different sea creatures. Watch the giant Pacific octopus make its way through clear tubes.

Get up close and personal with seals and otters in the open-air areas. Watch them eat, sleep, or feed their young. Then get your hands wet at the Life on the Edge exhibit. The tide pool is home to sea creatures from the Puget Sound. Reach in! You can touch real hermit crabs, sea cucumbers, and sea urchins.

Pet sea stars at the Seattle Aquarium's Life on the Edge exhibit.

The giant Pacific octopus is just one of the many sea creatures you'll see at the Seattle Aquarium.

MUSEUM OF FLIGHT

> Next, take off to the Museum of Flight in Seattle. It's one of the largest air and space museums in the world. Check out the collection of more than 150 aircraft. See what the first airplanes looked like! Trace how these early airplanes changed into what flies in the sky now. Then marvel at a model of the Apollo Command Module that went to the moon. You can even spy on the first Air Force One jet.

After looking around, put your hands on the controls. Climb in the pilot's seat of a fighter jet. Try out the many hands-on activities. Dock a spacecraft, or land a space shuttle on the moon. Then climb aboard a 737 airplane to watch movies about flight. Test your piloting skills at the Kid's Flight Zone. Strap yourself into a hang glider simulator. Then hop into a hot-air balloon basket or sit in the cockpit of a helicopter. Learn about aircraft controls. A wind machine shows how different aircraft fly in the sky.

End your visit by climbing to the top of the tower on Boeing Field's runway. Watch real planes take off and land. Listen up! You'll hear air traffic controllers. They talk to one another and pilots to keep the skies safe.

The first presidential Air Force One jet

Climb inside a real helicopter at the Museum of Flight!

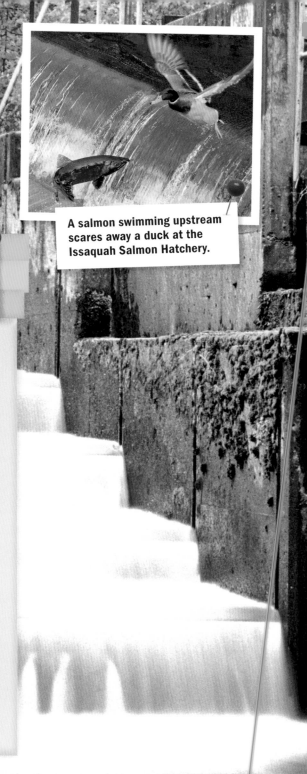

ISSAQUAH
SALMON HATCHERY

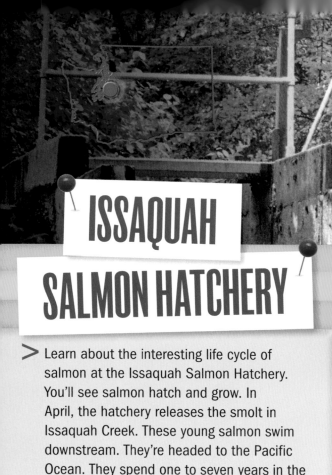

A salmon swimming upstream scares away a duck at the Issaquah Salmon Hatchery.

> Learn about the interesting life cycle of salmon at the Issaquah Salmon Hatchery. You'll see salmon hatch and grow. In April, the hatchery releases the smolt in Issaquah Creek. These young salmon swim downstream. They're headed to the Pacific Ocean. They spend one to seven years in the ocean. After the smolt have grown, they swim back upstream. They will spawn in the creek. In the fall, watch the many salmon jump the hatchery's ladder on their way home.

While you're at the hatchery, go on a tour. You can view a lighted map of the salmon's route. See aquariums filled with some of the 6 million salmon released every year. Come back the first weekend in October for the Issaquah Salmon Days Festival. There's something fishy for everyone. Watch a parade, listen to concerts, build crafts, and learn about salmon.

SAVING SALMON

Washington's waters were once filled with salmon. Thousands of people worked on salmon fishing boats. But wild salmon are becoming endangered. Overfishing and blocked migration paths are partly to blame. In 2005, the Washington State Senate passed Bill 5610. This bill set in motion ways to save the salmon. The Issaquah Salmon Hatchery helped restore some of the salmon paths. The hatchery brought back a place for the salmon to spawn.

SAN JUAN ISLANDS
WHALE WATCHING

> Head into Puget Sound to the San Juan Islands. Come in summer for an orca whale-watching trip. Take a ferry to Friday Harbor on San Juan Island. Then decide how close you want to get to the black and white giants.

Get closest to San Juan wildlife on a Crystal Seas Kayaking trip. Your guide will help you spot bald eagles, sea stars, seals, and maybe some orcas too! The only guaranteed way to see orcas is onboard the San Juan Excursions Whale Watching Cruises. Your next trip is free if you don't spot one. Listen as your guide drops a hydrophone overboard. This instrument lets you listen to the orcas call and whistle. Grab a pair of binoculars to watch the whales surface.

If you'd rather see whales from land, go to Lime Kiln Point State Park. This park is one of the best places in the world to see whales from shore. Also check out the park's orca displays and activities. Before leaving the island, visit the Whale Museum. Here you'll hear orcas communicate. Watch videos about them, and see real whale skeletons.

Three pods, or groups, of massive orca whales swim in the waters of Washington's San Juan Islands.

Get even closer to orcas on a Crystal Seas Kayaking trip.

CASCADE RANGE

> The Cascade Range in western Washington is peppered with volcanoes. Some are active. They could erupt at any time. But scientists are monitoring the volcanoes. Check out the destruction Mount Saint Helens caused. It erupted on May 18, 1980. Watch films of the explosion and walk through a volcano model at the Mount Saint Helens Forest Learning Center. Then hike to see the volcano and the wildlife that has returned to the area. Grab your flashlight and climb through Ape Cave.

Don't forget to visit Mount Rainier. It's the tallest volcano in the Cascade Range. And it's active! Steam escapes from its 2.7-mile-high (4.3 km) peak. But it's a safe place to hike, camp, fish, and picnic. Some trees here are one thousand years old. Smell the flowers in colorful meadows. Or visit in the winter to enjoy downhill skiing, snowshoeing, and sledding. Winter camping is an option if you dare. Guides will lead you on snowshoe treks. You can even become a Junior Ranger and earn a badge! All you have to do is visit and learn about the Cascades.

Ape Cave is the longest lava tube in the continental United States.

CHIEF SEATTLE

Before settlers moved west, American Indian nations lived in what is now Washington. They were divided into two groups. The nations that lived west of the Cascades caught seafood to eat and built homes from wood. The nations east of the Cascades were hunters and gatherers. They moved often in search of food. In 1805, Lewis and Clark arrived. They reported back east about the rich resources in the area. Soon, settlers arrived. A group of them founded Seattle in 1851. They named the settlement after American Indian chief Seattle. A statue of him stands in Seattle.

OLYMPIC NATIONAL PARK

> Visit three parks in one at the Olympic National Park. The park offers roughly 1,440 square miles (3,730 sq. km) to explore. Go from soggy rain forests to beaches to glacier-topped mountains. First, grab your raincoat and boots. You'll need them in the Hoh Rain Forest. This forest is part of the park. It receives 140 to 170 inches (356 to 432 centimeters) of rain each year. Hike past huge ferns and 200-foot-tall (61 m) trees covered in moss. Then head down to the rugged coast. Hunt for tiny garnets on Ruby Beach.

Next, visit the towering Olympic Mountains. During the summer, stop at Hurricane Ridge Visitor Center. Peer through a telescope. Can you see the glaciers on Mount Olympus? Then hike the trails to see waterfalls, wildlife, and meadows of wildflowers. Come back in the winter to enjoy ski runs and snowshoe trails.

WASHINGTON'S TIMBER

Trees once covered more than half of the Evergreen State. Washington's timber industry began in the mid-1800s. It quickly became the state's third-largest industry. Many people had jobs clearing trees and cutting timber. But years of cutting trees turned the forests into bare land. Many wild animals lost their homes. The environment suffered. Timber companies now plant new trees to help restore the areas they cut.

Tide pools on the coast of Olympic National Park are full of crabs, sea stars, and sea urchins.

GOLDENDALE OBSERVATORY STATE PARK

> Become starstruck at the Goldendale Observatory State Park in Goldendale. A 24.5-inch (62 cm) telescope sits at the top of a hill. It is one of the largest telescopes open to the public in the United States. Peer into the telescope to gaze into space. The telescope is so powerful you can see the moon, stars, or Jupiter.

During the day, you might be able to see bright stars and planets, such as Venus. Check out displays of the planets while you wait for the sun to set. After sunset, the scientists will help you view the moon, the planets, and the stars. Don't forget to bring a camera! Snap your own pictures of the moon or the stars. Each telescope has a holder for your camera.

Scientists at the Goldendale Observatory help point the giant telescope into space.

Use the telescope to see the sun's swirling gases.

The laser show at the Grand Coulee Dam highlights the history of the Columbia River with fun, colorful designs.

GRAND COULEE DAM

> The Grand Coulee Dam spans the Columbia River. The dam is 1 mile (1.6 km) wide. Take a tour of the dam to see what's hiding inside. A glass elevator takes you past some of the world's largest generators. When you're done with your tour, check out the exhibits at the Visitor Center. A virtual reality game will take you on a fly-through tour of the dam. Or operate a real jackhammer! You can hold onto it and turn it on. Feel it vibrate and pretend you're helping build the dam.

Head outside to visit Lake Roosevelt. It was created when the dam plugged up the river. The lake is a great place to boat, fish, and swim. And its shore offers a perfect place for camping and hiking. If you visit in summer, stick around for a laser light show. It's projected onto the dam and lasts thirty minutes.

WATERING WASHINGTON

The Grand Coulee Dam was built from 1933 to 1942. It brought water from the Columbia River to the dry desertlike areas in east Washington. Today it provides water for more than 650,000 acres (263,000 hectares) of farmland each year. The dam is also the biggest producer of waterpower in the United States.

SPOKANE

RIVER RAFTING

> Are you a thrill-seeker? Then head to Spokane and check out the Spokane River. Grab a paddle and a life jacket and go whitewater rafting. A guide will help your group paddle through waves and over rocks! Paddle past rock formations and pine trees. Maybe you'll spy an eagle flying overhead.

Or if you're looking for a more relaxing ride on the water, try a float trip. Row Adventure Center offers float trips all summer long. Take a lazy ride on the 5-mile-long (8 km) river. Float along in a raft and enjoy the sunshine. There are mellow "pools" along the way. Jump on in when you get warm. For a little more action, choose a kayak instead.

Paddle your way down the Spokane River in a kayak.

Be ready to get wet if you choose to raft down the river!

YOUR TOP TEN

You've just read about ten awesome things to see and do in Washington. Now it's your turn! If you visited Washington, what would be on your top ten list? What places in Washington do you look forward to visiting? Grab a sheet of paper and jot down your Washington top ten list. You could even make your list into a book. Add your own drawings or pictures from the Internet.

WASHINGTON BY MAP

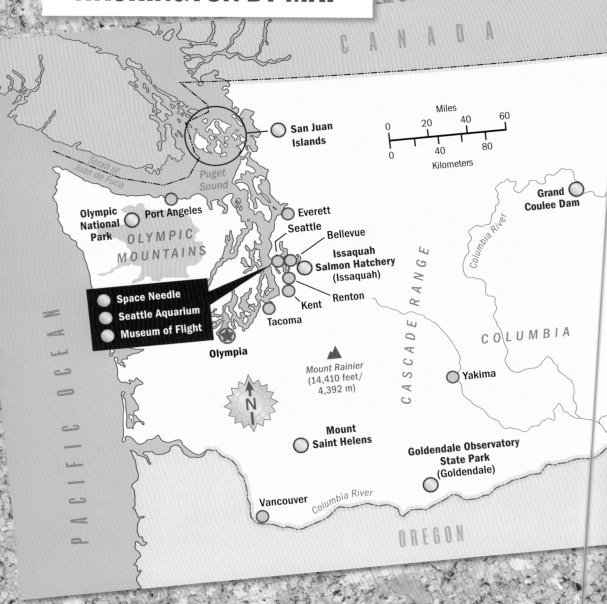

CANADA

Miles
0   20   40   60

0   40   80
Kilometers

San Juan Islands

Strait of Juan de Fuca

Puget Sound

Grand Coulee Dam

Columbia River

Olympic National Park

Port Angeles

OLYMPIC MOUNTAINS

Everett

Seattle

Bellevue

Issaquah Salmon Hatchery (Issaquah)

- Space Needle
- Seattle Aquarium
- Museum of Flight

Kent   Renton

Tacoma

Olympia

CASCADE RANGE

COLUMBIA

Mount Rainier (14,410 feet/ 4,392 m)

N

PACIFIC OCEAN

Yakima

Mount Saint Helens

Goldendale Observatory State Park (Goldendale)

Vancouver   Columbia River

OREGON

ROCKY
MOUNTAINS

Spokane River

Spokane
Valley

Spokane

IDAHO

PLATEAU

Snake River

Walla Walla

BLUE MOUNTAINS

> MAP KEY

⭐ Capital city

◯ City

◎ Point of interest

▲ Highest elevation

-··- International border

-·- State border

THE SEAL OF THE STATE OF WASHINGTON 1889

Visit www.lerneresource.com to learn
more about the state flag of Washington.

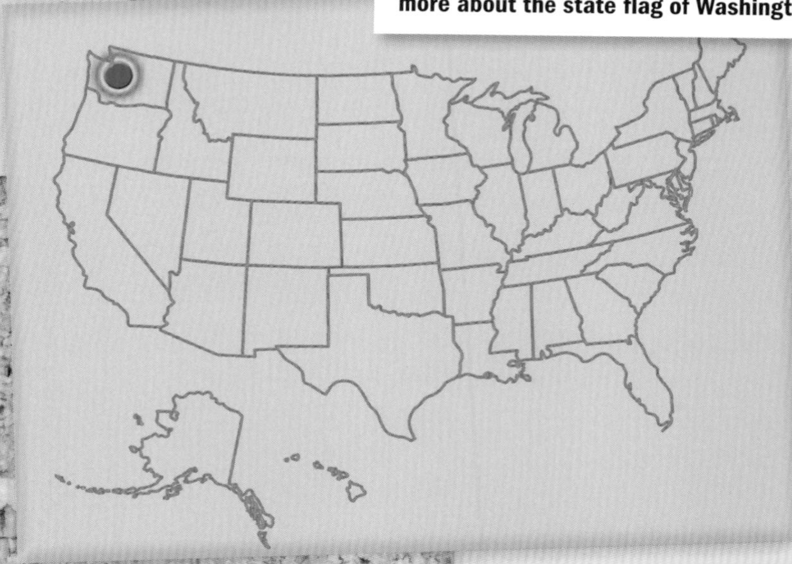

WASHINGTON FACTS

NICKNAME: Evergreen State

SONG: "Washington, My Home" by Helen Davis

MOTTO: *Al-Ki* (Chinook word for "by and by")

> **FLOWER:** coast rhododendron

TREE: western hemlock

> **BIRD:** willow goldfinch

ANIMALS: orca whale, steelhead trout

> **FOOD:** apple

DATE AND RANK OF STATEHOOD: November 11, 1889; the 42nd state

CAPITAL: Olympia

AREA: 68,095 square miles (176,365 sq. km)

AVERAGE JANUARY TEMPERATURE: 30°F (–1°C)

AVERAGE JULY TEMPERATURE: 66°F (19°C)

POPULATION AND RANK: 6,971,406; 13th (2013)

MAJOR CITIES AND POPULATIONS: Seattle (634,535), Spokane (209,525), Tacoma (202,010), Vancouver (165,489), Bellevue (126,439)

NUMBER OF US CONGRESS MEMBERS: 10 representatives; 2 senators

NUMBER OF ELECTORAL VOTES: 12

> **NATURAL RESOURCES:** timber, coal, copper, gold, lead, limestone, silver, salmon

AGRICULTURAL PRODUCTS: wheat, apples, dry peas, corn, soybeans, cherries, potatoes, raspberries, lentils, hay, beef cattle, flower bulbs, milk, timber

MANUFACTURED GOODS: aircraft, spacecraft, circuits, aluminum, ships, electronics, software, chemicals, computer equipment, paper products, lumber

STATE HOLIDAYS AND CELEBRATIONS: Issaquah Salmon Days, Washington State Spring Fair, SummerFest, Edmonds Waterfront Festival

GLOSSARY

endangered: in danger of becoming extinct

garnet: a dark red stone used in jewelry

generator: a machine that produces electricity

hatchery: a place where humans raise fish or chickens from eggs

hydrophone: an instrument used to listen to sounds going through water

migration: the movement of animals from one area to another at a certain time of year

monorail: a type of railroad that runs on a single track, high off the ground

observatory: a building with telescopes for studying the stars and weather

simulator: a machine that imitates conditions to allow you to experience a place or task

smolt: a young salmon that migrates to the sea for the first time

spawn: to produce eggs

LERNER

SOURCE

Expand learning beyond the printed book. Download free, complementary educational resources for this book from our website, www.lerneresource.com.

FURTHER INFORMATION

National Geographic Kids—Orcas
http://kids.nationalgeographic.com/animals/orca.html
Learn fun facts, see and hear videos, e-mail greeting cards, and print
a collector card about orca whales.

National Park Service—Web Rangers Activities
http://www.nps.gov/webrangers/search.cfm
Play games and do puzzles to learn more about Washington's history, nature,
people, animals, and parks.

PBS—Grand Coulee Dam
http://www.pbs.org/wgbh/buildingbig/wonder/structure/grand_coulee.html
Learn fun facts about the dam, how it was built, and how it compares to
other dams.

Pratt, Laura. *Washington*. New York: AV2 by Weigl, 2013. Read about more fun
things to do in Washington!

Schuetz, Kristin. *Washington: The Evergreen State*. Minneapolis: Bellwether
Media, 2014. This book introduces readers to Washington's geography
and culture.

Silverman, Buffy. *How Do Jets Work?* Minneapolis: Lerner Publications, 2013.
Learn more about the kinds of jets you will find at the Museum of Flight!

INDEX

PHOTO ACKNOWLEDGMENTS

The images in this book are used with the permission of: © Robert Crum /Thinkstock, p. 1; NASA, pp. 2–3; © Spirit of America/Shutterstock Images, pp. 4, 17 (right); © Monika Wieland /Shutterstock Images, pp. 4–5, 15 (left); © Laura Westlund/Independent Picture Service, pp. 5, 26–27; © Shutterstock Images, pp. 6, 24, 29 (top right), 29 (top left), 29 (bottom right), 29 (bottom left); Carol M. Highsmith Archive/Library of Congress, pp. 6–7 (LC-DIG-highsm-04423), 23 (LC-DIG-highsm-12109); © incamerastoc/Alamy, p. 7; © Chuck Pefley/Alamy, p. 8; © dk /Alamy, pp. 8–9; © Jason Mintzer /Shutterstock Images, p. 9; Public Domain, pp. 10–11; © Ian Dagnall Commercial Collection/Alamy, p. 11 (top), 11 (bottom); © CB2/ZOB /Wenn.com/Newscom, p. 12; © Zach Holmes/Alamy, pp. 12–13; © Stanislav Komogorov/Shutterstock Images, p. 13; © Natalia Bratslavsky/Shutterstock Images, pp. 14–15; © Martin Mark Soerensen/Thinkstock, p. 15 (right); © tusharkoley/Shutterstock Images, pp. 16–17; © Tom Uhlman/Alamy, p. 17 (left); © Mares Lucian/Shutterstock Images, p. 18; © Stanislav Moroz /Thinkstock, pp. 18–19; National Park Service, p. 19; Robert Gendler/NASA, pp. 20–21; A. Balet, p. 21 (top); SDO /NASA, p. 21 (bottom); © Kevin Schafer/Alamy, p. 22; © Chris Boswell /Thinkstock, pp. 22–23; © Thinkstock, pp. 24–25, 25; © nicoolay/iStockphoto, p. 27.

Cover: © Beboy_ltd/iStock/Thinkstock (Seattle skyline); © Blueenayim /Dreamstime.com (starfish); © Monika Wieland/Shutterstock.com (orca whale); photo courtesy of Peak 7 Adventures www.peak7.org (rafting); © Laura Westlund/Independent Picture Service (map); © iStockphoto.com/fpm (seal); © iStockphoto.com/vicm (pushpins); © iStockphoto.com/benz190 (corkboard).